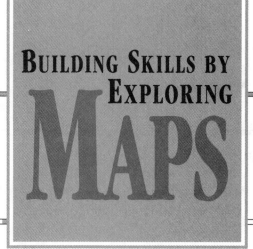

BUILDING SKILLS BY EXPLORING
MAPS

The World

Written and Edited by
Alaska Hults

Illustrator: Mapping Specialists
Cover Illustrator: Rick Grayson
Designer: Barbara Peterson
Cover Designer: Barbara Peterson
Art Director: Tom Cochrane
Project Director: Carolea Williams

Table of Contents

Introduction

 The wonderful thing about teaching students map skills is that they really want to know how to read maps. To students maps are keys to unknown places. Maps hold the promise of an adventure.

Middle-elementary students understand that maps represent places. However, they do not have much experience making inferences from maps. They assume north is straight up, and they become confused by over-crowded maps. The maps in *The World* provide an excellent bridge to a much deeper understanding of map reading by eliminating extra details—but not so many that the map loses all context.

As students work with the maps in *The World,* they will

- explain and use the coordinate grid system of latitude and longitude to determine the absolute locations of places on Earth.

- read and interpret thematic maps.

- estimate distances between two places on a map, using a scale of miles, and use cardinal and ordinal directions when referring to relative location.

- know world patterns of resource distribution and utilization.

- use a variety of maps and documents to identify physical and culture features of neighborhoods, cities, states, and countries.

- obtain information about a topic using a variety of visual sources such as pictures, symbols, and maps.

You do not have to use the maps in this book in order. Full lessons on each culture or place are not provided. Supplement difficult concepts with lessons from your social studies curriculum. Schedule about 20 minutes for each map experience. Invite students to bring in maps they find, and have the class examine them. Have the class find the title, key, scale, compass rose, and lines of latitude and longitude on the map.

Invite students to compare the maps to other maps of the same places. Have them discuss where they see concentrations of settlements. Invite them to place older maps side by side with current maps to observe changes in a region over time. If they spend enough time with the maps and activity sheets, they will better retain the names and locations of the places they read about or hear about in the news. Conveniently, the skills will also transfer well to a standardized-testing situation.

How to Use This Book

Hitting the Map Standards

Before you have students read and complete the activity page that precedes each map, lay a firm foundation for the activity by having students complete the Evaluate the Map reproducible (page 5). This reproducible will keep students' map skills sharp for test-taking and will better prepare them to think critically as they complete the activity page that accompanies the map. The first few times that students evaluate a map, guide them through completing the reproducible. Copy the map to an overhead transparency, and display it, so you can point to specific elements of the map during discussion. You may want to use the following tips as you do so.

1. Have students work in pairs the first time they complete the reproducible. More details are identified when two pairs of eyes examine the same map.

2. Have a volunteer read aloud the directions. Emphasize that students should be as complete as possible in their answers. This is especially important for questions 7, 8, and 10.

3. Students may simply copy the title for question 1. For question 2, they should not repeat the information in the title. Have them carefully examine the map and ask the following questions:

   • This map was created by a person. What was the person trying to show or teach in this map?

   • Is there a lot of general information or a little, very specific information?

   • Is there anything here that seems out of place? What is it and why do you think the mapmaker included it?

4. Students may need a thorough review of the map terms before they can complete question 3. Assign a color to each check box, and have students circle or underline the parts of the map that correspond to each check box. Invite volunteers to complete this step on the overhead map.

5. Students will benefit from handling a globe for question 4. Help students find the lines of latitude and longitude. Have them notice the direction abbreviation after each measurement. Have them find North America. Point out that North America is in the Northern and Western hemispheres. Model how to relate the map to an area on the globe using latitude and longitude. These maps were produced with a variety of projections to minimize distortion, but land closer to the poles will still show some distortion. Point out any discrepancies you see between the flat maps and the globe.

6. For question 5, help students picture the edge of the map as a number line and the intersecting lines of latitude or longitude as points on the number line. Help them estimate the approximate measurement of the points at each corner.

7. For question 6, model how to use a ruler to understand the scale. The activity sheets will provide more practice with using the scale to find actual distances. If students struggle with the scale, have them use the ruler to add additional hatch marks to it.

8. For questions 7, 8, and 9, students may simply look at the map and copy the appropriate titles for each item. Question 9 will not always have a visibly obvious answer. Accept all reasonable estimates.

9. Question 10 is fairly self-explanatory. You may invite students to pick four symbols to describe if the key is very detailed and time is short.

Evaluate the Map

Use the map to answer the questions.

1. What is the title of the map?_____

2. What does the map aim to convey?_____

3. Check the box. This map . . .

   ❏ shows political boundaries.

   ❏ shows land and water features.

   ❏ has a key.

   ❏ has a scale.

   ❏ includes a compass rose.

   ❏ has grid lines.

   ❏ has lines of latitude and longitude.

   ❏ shows individual towns or cities.

   ❏ includes information specific to the. people who live there such as the. kinds of business conducted, level. of education, or locations of conflict.

4. What hemisphere(s) are shown in part or full on the map?_____

5. Use what you know about latitude and longitude to estimate the following:
   This map spans from _____ to _____ latitude and from _____ to _____ longitude.

6. Align the zero on a ruler with the edge of the scale. Describe the scale in terms of inches and miles or centimeters and kilometers (e.g., The scale is 500 miles for each 1.5 inches.). _____
   _____
   _____

7. List some of the land features that are labeled on the map.

8. List four water features that are labeled on the map.

9. Which body of water appears to cover the greatest area? _____

10. Describe the key. What symbols are shown? How do they help you understand the information on the map? _____
    _____
    _____
    _____

Using the Activity Pages

Each activity page contains a short section with enough information about the place featured on the map for students to put what they see in context. Knowing more about the history or people of a location also provides them with mental "hooks" that help them remember what they see.

The activity pages contain either ten questions to which students will respond, or six multiple-choice questions similar to those found on standardized tests. These ten questions include those that address coordinates in latitude and longitude, scale, direction relative to a location, reading the key, and relating the map to the background information provided on each page.

Latitude and Longitude

The challenge at this level is that the students' ability to read the map is strong enough that they would rather hunt for a location than use latitude and longitude to find it. Because of this, each activity page has at least two questions that require students to use this skill. They are asked to find a location using given coordinates. Then, they are asked to estimate the coordinates of a given location. The answer key provides a possible response. You will need to determine the skill level of your students and the scale of the map to decide the margin of error. Students with a great deal of map experience may be asked to be more exact than students who are just learning. The skill of estimating map coordinates is actually fairly complex—students must be able to determine the difference between the two nearest lines (e.g., Are there five degrees between lines? Ten? Fifteen?), and then they must divide the space between those lines into equal areas to find, essentially, each degree between the lines. Finally, if the scale is fairly large, they may need to estimate the distance between each degree. In this book, most coordinates were rounded to the nearest degree. There are a few exceptions where it was rounded to the nearest half degree.

Scale

Although this is a difficult concept for students, once they grasp it they want to measure everything. As with latitude and longitude, provide students new to the skill with a greater margin of error. All of the distances on this map were estimated using one of the two following methods and are not intended to replace any figures you might see listed in a detailed index of modern cities.

Method One—Give each student a blank index card. Have students align the top left corner of the card with the left edge of the scale. Have them use a pencil to copy the hatch marks of the scale and their labels onto the top edge of the card. Have them move the card so that the last hatch mark aligns with the first mark of the scale and extend the scale on their card to double its length. Students should calculate the new distances and add those to their scale. If hatch marks are more than $1/4$" apart, have them use a ruler to divide the area between hatch marks into smaller equal sections. Have them calculate the value of each of the new hatch marks and add that to their scale. This will facilitate more accurate estimates of distance. Then, have them measure distance by aligning the left edge of the card with the center of the first point and then rotating the card until the edge of it passes through the center of the second point. Students should then use the scale on

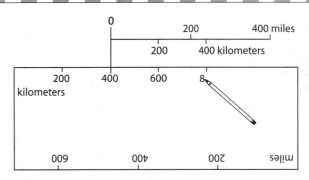

the edge of the card to estimate the distance. This is an easy and effective way to measure more than one location. Extend the activity by having students copy miles onto one edge of the card and kilometers onto the other.

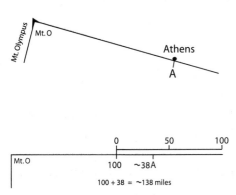

Method Two—Give each student a blank index card. Have students align the left corner of the card with the center of the first point. Have them rotate the card until the edge of it passes through the center of the second point. Then, have them mark the location of the second place on the edge of the card. Finally, have them align the edge of the card with the scale and compare to find the distance. If the distance exceeds the length of the scale on the map, have them make a small mark to show the end of the scale, move that mark back to zero, and measure the remaining distance. Then, students add the two distances together to find the total distance. This is an easy and effective way to measure one distance.

Cardinal and Ordinal Directions

The cardinal directions are north, south, east, and west. Ordinal directions are these points: northwest, northeast, southwest, and southeast. Help students understand these directions further by using a compass to find north in your own classroom. While students usually quickly master the names of the directions and their relationships to each other, they still struggle to apply those directions to one place on a map in relation to another. An interesting cultural note: Saying the directions in the order of north, south, east, and west is a "western" tradition. Many cultures use a different order. For example, the Navajo always start with east and continue clockwise to north. Ask your second-language learners how they learned the directions. Taking a moment to discuss them may help students connect the "old" directions to the "new" ones.

Mapping the Modern World

While the maps in this book are a great start for exploring the world, students should be given an opportunity to explore further. Consider bringing in a variety of road atlases for students to look through. Include atlases that show entire regions as well as travel guides that show a single city in incredible detail. Online map generators are also a fun way for students to explore their own and distant communities.

Name_____ **Date**_____

Africa

Read the paragraph for background information. Then use the map to answer the questions.

Did you know? Africa is home to three of the largest rivers on Earth: the Nile, the Congo, and the Niger rivers. The continent's enormous river systems could potentially provide an almost unlimited source of hydroelectric power.

1. Which three capital cities sit on or nearly on the equator?

   _____   _____   _____

2. Which two rivers feed into the Nile River?

   _____   _____

3. The Congo River crosses the equator in two places. What is special about this river?

   _____

4. Which city is at 5°S and 30°E?   _____

5. What is the approximate location in latitude and longitude of the city
   of Lusaka in Zambia?   _____

6. Which capital city is directly south of Asmara, Eritrea?   _____

7. If you walked northwest along the coast from Monrovia, Liberia, which other capital cities would you
   pass on your way to Dakar, Senegal?

   _____   _____   _____   _____

8. Which city is probably closer to Gaborone, Botswana: Windhoek,
   Namibia or Harare, Zimbabwe?   _____

9. Approximately how far is it from Algiers to Tripoli?   _____

10. Name two countries that share the Sahara desert.

    _____   _____

Maps: *The World* © 2005 Creative Teaching Press

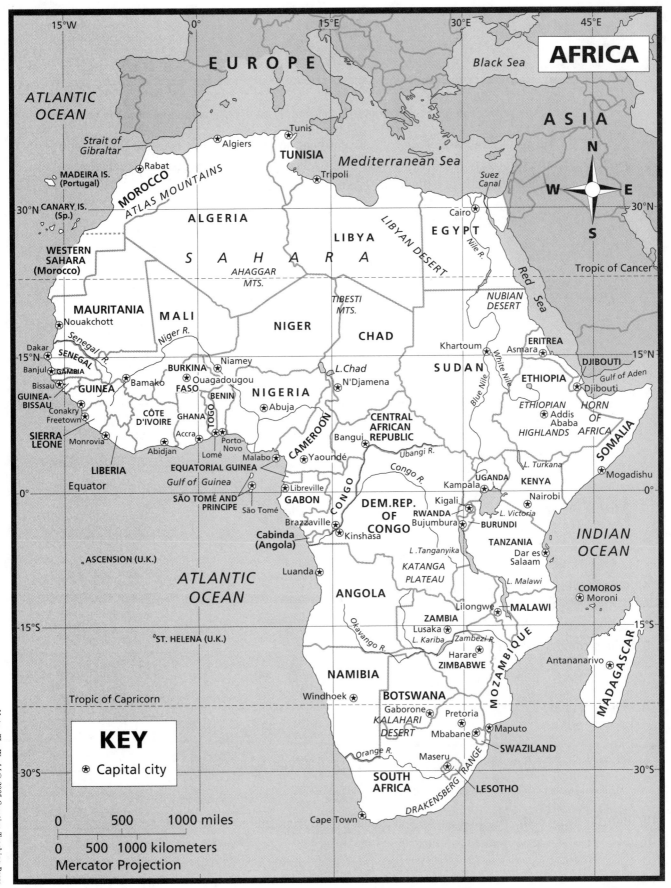

AFRICA

15°W 0° 15°E 30°E 45°E

EUROPE

Black Sea

ATLANTIC OCEAN

ASIA

Strait of Gibraltar

Tunis

Algiers

TUNISIA

Mediterranean Sea

Suez Canal

N
W   E
S

MADEIRA IS. (Portugal)

Rabat

MOROCCO

Tripoli

ATLAS MOUNTAINS

Cairo

30°N

CANARY IS. (Sp.)

ALGERIA

LIBYA

LIBYAN DESERT

EGYPT

Nile R.

30°N

Tropic of Cancer

WESTERN SAHARA (Morocco)

S A H A R A

AHAGGAR MTS.

TIBESTI MTS.

Red Sea

NUBIAN DESERT

MAURITANIA

MALI

NIGER

CHAD

Khartoum

Asmara

ERITREA

15°N

Nouakchott

Niger R.

SUDAN

White Nile

DJIBOUTI

Gulf of Aden

15°N

Dakar

Senegal R.

Niamey

SENEGAL

Banjul

GAMBIA

Bamako

Ouagadougou

BURKINA FASO

N'Djamena

L.Chad

NIGERIA

Abuja

CENTRAL AFRICAN REPUBLIC

Blue Nile

ETHIOPIA

ETHIOPIAN HIGHLANDS

Addis Ababa

Djibouti

HORN OF AFRICA

Bissau

GUINEA-BISSAU

GUINEA

Conakry

BENIN

TOGO

GHANA

CÔTE D'IVOIRE

Accra

Freetown

SIERRA LEONE

Monrovia

Abidjan

Lomé

Porto-Novo

Bangui

Ubangi R.

Yaoundé

CAMEROON

L. Turkana

SOMALIA

Mogadishu

LIBERIA

Equator

EQUATORIAL GUINEA

Gulf of Guinea

Malabo

Congo R.

UGANDA

Kampala

KENYA

Nairobi

0°

SÃO TOMÉ AND PRINCIPE

São Tomé

Libreville

GABON

CONGO

DEM. REP. OF CONGO

Kigali

RWANDA

Bujumbura

BURUNDI

L. Victoria

0°

Brazzaville

Kinshasa

Cabinda (Angola)

TANZANIA

Dar es Salaam

INDIAN OCEAN

ASCENSION (U.K.)

L.Tanganyika

KATANGA PLATEAU

ATLANTIC OCEAN

Luanda

L. Malawi

COMOROS

Moroni

ANGOLA

Lilongwe

MALAWI

ST. HELENA (U.K.)

ZAMBIA

Lusaka

15°S

Okavango R.

L. Kariba

Zambezi R.

15°S

Tropic of Capricorn

NAMIBIA

Harare

ZIMBABWE

Antananarivo

MADAGASCAR

MOZAMBIQUE

Windhoek

BOTSWANA

KEY

Capital city

Gaborone

Pretoria

KALAHARI DESERT

Mbabane

Maputo

SWAZILAND

Orange R.

Maseru

DRAKENSBERG RANGE

LESOTHO

30°S

SOUTH AFRICA

30°S

0 500 1000 miles

0 500 1000 kilometers

Mercator Projection

Cape Town

Asia

Read the paragraph for background information. Then use the map to answer the questions.

Did you know? Asia is the largest continent on Earth. Its name is so old that no one really knows its origins. All of the world's major religions originated in Asia. These include Buddhism, Christianity, Hinduism, Islam, and Judaism.

1. Is Hong Kong the capital of China? How can you tell?

_____

2. What other continents directly touch Asia? _____ _____

3. How does the map clarify the difference between an island name, such as Sumatra, and a country name, such as Indonesia?

_____

4. Which sea lies along the 60th meridian in the Eastern Hemisphere? _____

5. What is the approximate location in latitude and longitude of Colombo, Sri Lanka? _____

6. Which capital city is NW of Beijing? _____

7. Which country is SE of Pakistan? _____

8. Which capital city is closest to Vientiane, Laos? _____

9. Which city is farthest from Baghdad: Ankara, Turkey, or Riyadh, Saudi Arabia? _____

10. How far away is the city that answers question 9 from Baghdad? _____

Maps: The World © 2005 Creative Teaching Press

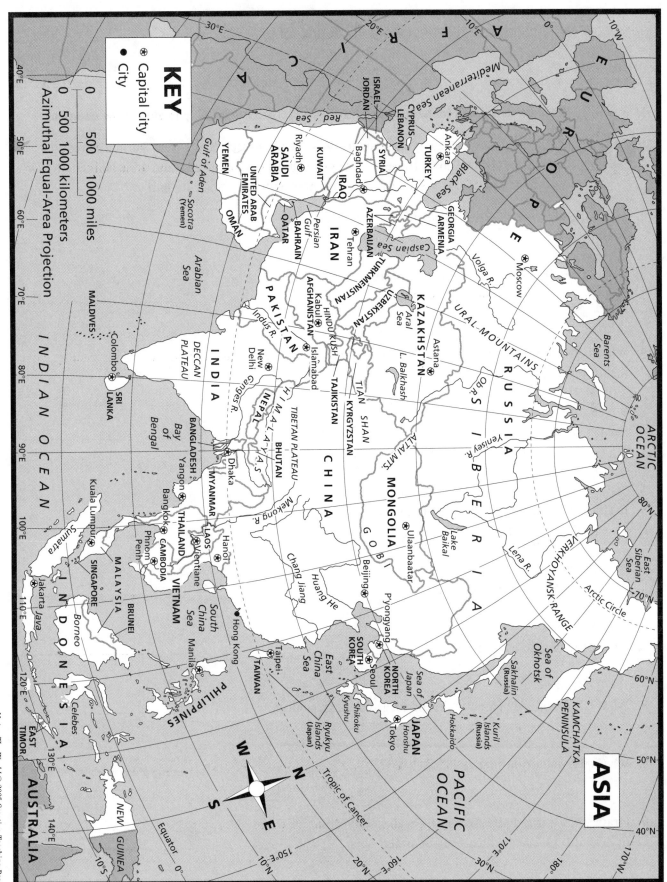

KEY
- ⊛ Capital city
- • City

Azimuthal Equal-Area Projection

0 500 1000 kilometers
0 500 1000 miles

ASIA

Maps: The World © 2005 Creative Teaching Press

Mexico

Read the paragraph for background information. Then use the map to answer the questions.

Did you know? The city of Acapulco was the only place in the New World allowed to receive Spanish galleons. The galleons held spices, silks, ivory, jade, and porcelain. These riches were tempting for pirates, and a large fort was built to protect the harbor.

1. Which city is closest to the Tropic of Cancer?

_____

2. Approximately how much distance lies between Parícutin Volcano and Orizaba?

_____

3. What is the capital of Mexico?

_____

4. Which direction do you travel from the Caribbean Sea to the Gulf of Tehuantepec?

_____

5. You are in San Luis Potosí. Which trip is shorter: to the Gulf of Mexico or the Pacific Ocean?

_____

6. If you live in Tijuana, which direction would take you to Cape San Lucas?

_____

7. Name the ruin closest to Cancún.

_____

8. What is the approximate latitude and longitude of Acapulco?

_____

9. What city would you find at 28°N and 107°W?

_____

10. Pirate ships trying to steal from the Spanish galleons in Acapulco sailed in which body of water?

_____

Maps: *The World* © 2005 Creative Teaching Press

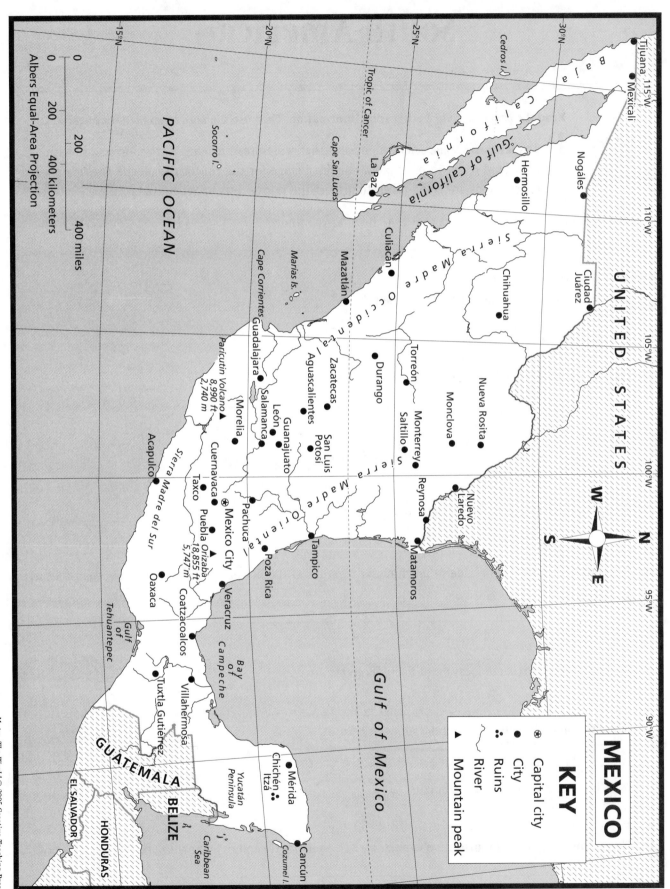

MEXICO

KEY

⊛ Capital city
● City
∴ Ruins
⌇ River
▲ Mountain peak

UNITED STATES

PACIFIC OCEAN

Gulf of Mexico

Gulf of California

Baja California

Sierra Madre Occidental

Sierra Madre Oriental

Sierra Madre del Sur

Tropic of Cancer

Cedros I.

Socorro I.

Marías Is.

Cape Corrientes

Cape San Lucas

Tijuana
Mexicali
Nogáles
Hermosillo
Ciudad Juárez
Chihuahua
La Paz
Culiacán
Mazatlán
Durango
Torreón
Monclova
Nueva Rosita
Monterrey
Saltillo
Reynosa
Nuevo Laredo
Matamoros
Zacatecas
Aguascalientes
San Luis Potosí
Guadalajara
León
Guanajuato
Salamanca
Morelia
Paricutín Volcano
8,990 ft
2,740 m
Acapulco
Cuernavaca
Taxco
Pachuca
Mexico City
Puebla
Orizaba
18,855 ft
5,747 m
Oaxaca
Coatzacoalcos
Veracruz
Poza Rica
Tampico
Gulf of Tehuantepec
Bay of Campeche
Tuxtla Gutiérrez
Villahermosa
Yucatán Peninsula
Mérida
Chichén Itzá
Cancún
Cozumel I.
Caribbean Sea

GUATEMALA
BELIZE
EL SALVADOR
HONDURAS

N
S
W
E

0   200   400 kilometers
0   200   400 miles

Albers Equal-Area Projection

South America

Read the paragraph for background information. Then use the map to answer the questions.

Did you know? Some scientists believe that widespread damage to the forests of South America could result in permanent climate change for the rest of the planet. For this reason and others, steps are being taken to protect the rain forests of South America.

1. Is São Paulo along the coast a capital city? How do you know?

   _____

2. Is Santiago, Chile a capital city? How do you know?

   _____

3. Name two rivers that feed into the Amazon River.

   _____   _____

4. What important ecological feature is located in Brazil?   _____

5. Which special line of latitude is located at 23.5˚S?   _____

6. Why are the lines of longitude so much closer together at the bottom portion of the map than they are at the top?

   _____

7. What is the approximate location of Sucre, Bolivia?   _____

8. Which capital city sits almost exactly on the equator?   _____

9. Which town is NE of Salvador, Brazil?   _____

10. To go from Bolivia's administrative capital, La Paz, to its legal capital, Sucre, how far would you travel?

    _____

Maps: *The World* © 2005 Creative Teaching Press

SOUTH AMERICA

Caribbean Sea

ATLANTIC

OCEAN

Pt. Gallinas

Cristóbal Colón
5,775 m

Caracas

**TRINIDAD &
TOBAGO**

10°N

Lake Maracaibo

VENEZUELA

Georgetown
Paramaribo

10°N

Orinoco R.

GUIANA HIGHLANDS

GUYANA

Cayenne

Bogotá

SURINAME

**FRENCH GUIANA
(Fr.)**

*Gulf
of
Panama*

Magdalena R.

LLANOS

COLOMBIA

Marajó Island

Equator

Negro R.

0°

Quito

Putumayo R.

A M A Z O N

0°

ECUADOR

Marañón R.

Amazon R.

S E L V A S

Madeira R.

Amazon R.

Xingu R.

Cape
São Roque

Pt. Pariñas

Juruá R.

B A S I N

Araguaia R.

Recife

Ucayali R.

São Francisco R.

Mt. Huascarán
6,768 m

P E R U

B R A Z I L

10°S

10°S

Lima

B R A Z I L I A N

Salvador

Lake Titicaca

Mamoré R.

La Paz

*MATO GROSSO
PLATEAU*

Brasília

H I G H L A N D S

BOLIVIA

Lake Poopó

Sucre

Paraguay R.

20°S

A T A C A M A   D E S E R T

PARAGUAY

Paraná R.

Rio de Janeiro

20°S

G R A N   C H A C O

Pilcomayo R.

Asunción

São Paulo

Tropic of Capricorn

Salado R.

Paraná R.

PACIFIC

Uruguay R.

OCEAN

Mt. Aconcagua
6,960 m

ARGENTINA

URUGUAY

Patos Lagoon

30°S

Santiago

P A M P A S

Buenos Aires

Montevideo

ATLANTIC

30°S

Colorado R.

Rio de la Plata

OCEAN

C H I L E

A N D E S

San Mateo Gulf

Chiloé Island

P A T A G O N I A

Valdés
Peninsula

KEY

Chonos Arch.

Gulf of San Jorge
Cape Tres Puntas

⊛ Capital city

40°S

40°S

Wellington
Island

● City

▲ Mountain

Strait of
Magellan

**Falkland
Islands
(U.K.)**

0   500   1000 miles

Tierra del
Fuego

0   500   1000 kilometers

Cape Horn

Azimuthal Equal-Area Projection

Europe

Read the paragraph for background information. Then use the map to answer the questions.

Did you know? The only continent smaller than Europe is Australia, but Europe is heavily populated. The region may owe some of its popularity to its access to water. Although the continent has few large lakes, it is home to a vast and complex system of rivers, and the coast is accessible to an innumerable quantity of bays, inlets, fjords, seas, and other bodies of water. With so much water around, the region was easy to travel through by boat, and it was a good place to grow crops and raise animals for food.

1. Which of the following is not part of Europe:
   Western Russia, Northern Africa, or Iceland? _____

2. Why was Europe a popular place for human settlement?

   _____

3. What is the approximate location in latitude and longitude
   of St. Petersburg, Russia? _____

4. Which city is located at 50°N and 15°E? _____

5. What two countries are found on the Iberian Peninsula? _____

6. Which sea is north of Albania? _____

7. In which direction must you travel to go from
   Athens, Greece to Tirana, Albania? _____

8. If a plane flew from Dublin, Ireland to London, England,
   about how far would it travel? _____

9. Which city is closer to Zagreb, Croatia: Sarajevo, Bosnia or
   Belgrade, Serbia-Montenegro? _____

10. Which countries border the Gulf of Bothnia? _____

Maps: *The World* © 2005 Creative Teaching Press

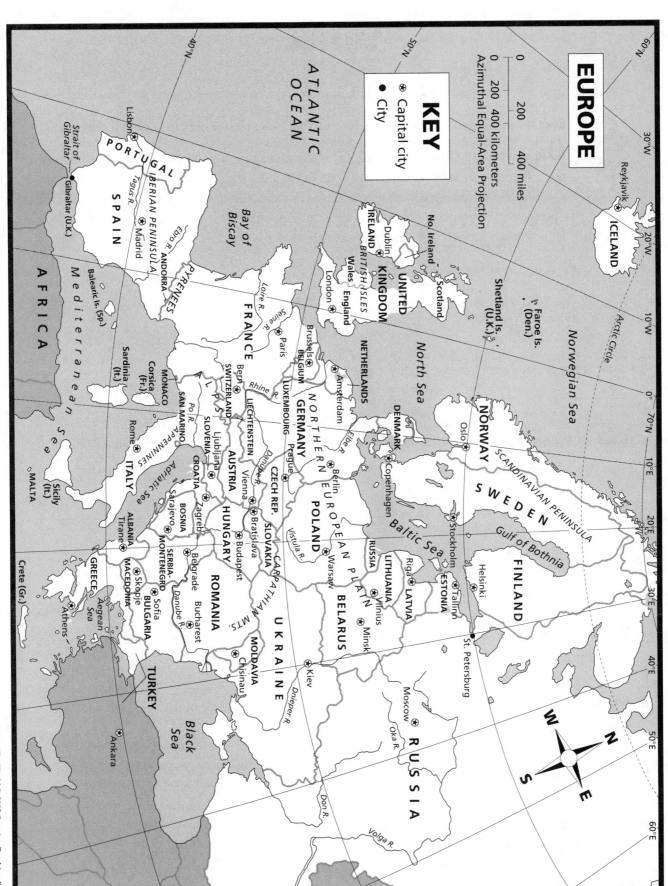

EUROPE

Europe 17

China

N
W ✦ **E**
S

Read the paragraph for background information. Then use the map to answer the questions.

Did you know? China is so big that it is almost as big as all of Europe. More people live there than in any other country on Earth. In the northeast corner of the country the land is dry and cold. In the southwest corner of the country there is a tropical monsoon climate. One out of every five people on the planet is Chinese. China is so large that there are still vast areas that are nearly uninhabited. These regions are less suited to human settlement.

1. Which special line of latitude is found at 23.5°N? _____

2. Which city would you find at approximately 36°N and 104°E? _____

3. What is the English name for the city of Xianggang (22°N, 114°E)? How do you know?
_____

4. Based on the reading, why might there be few major roads through the Tibetan Plateau?
_____

5. What is the approximate distance from Fuzhou to Nanchang? _____

6. If you wanted to get from Zengzhou (34°N, 114°E) to Hohhot (41°N, 112°E), through which city would you most likely pass? _____

7. What is the approximate location in latitude and longitude of Hangzhou? _____

8. Which city on the map seems farthest north? Is it really the city farthest north in China? Explain.
_____

9. Which city is southeast of Nanning (23°N, 108.5°E)? _____

10. If you sail north on the Yellow Sea from Yantai, at which city would you arrive? _____

Maps: The World © 2005 Creative Teaching Press

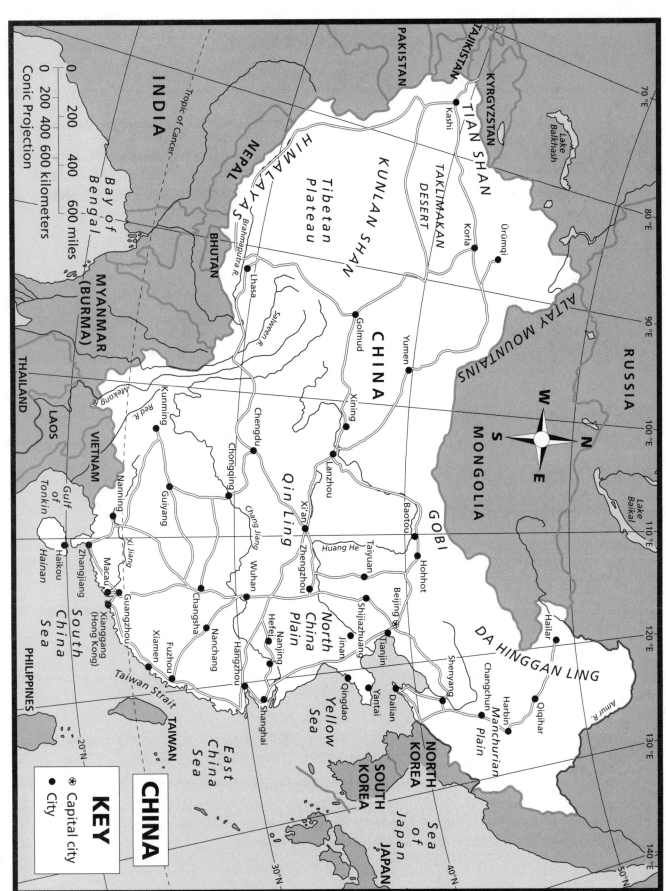

CHINA

KEY
⊕ Capital city
● City

INDIA
Bay of Bengal
Tropic of Cancer
MYANMAR (BURMA)
THAILAND
LAOS
VIETNAM
Gulf of Tonkin
South China Sea
PHILIPPINES
Taiwan Strait
TAIWAN
East China Sea
Hainan
Haikou
Zhanjiang
Macau
Xianggang (Hong Kong)
Guangzhou
Nanning
Xi Jiang
Fuzhou
Xiamen
Nanchang
Changsha
Hangzhou
Nanjing
Hefei
Shanghai
Wuhan
Yellow Sea
Qingdao
Yantai
Jinan
Shijiazhuang
Dalian
Shenyang
Changchun
Harbin
Qiqihar
Hailar
SOUTH KOREA
NORTH KOREA
Sea of Japan
JAPAN
Manchurian Plain
DA HINGGAN LING
Amur R.
Lake Baikal
RUSSIA
MONGOLIA
GOBI
Beijing
Tianjin
Hohhot
Baotou
Taiyuan
Huang He
Zhengzhou
North China Plain
Xi'an
Qin Ling
Chang Jiang
Chongqing
Guiyang
Kunming
Chengdu
Nanning
Red R.
Mekong R.
Lanzhou
Xining
Golmud
Yumen
CHINA
KUNLAN SHAN
Tibetan Plateau
Lhasa
Salween R.
Brahmaputra R.
HIMALAYAS
NEPAL
BHUTAN
TAKLIMAKAN DESERT
TIAN SHAN
Kashi
Korla
Ürümqi
KYRGYZSTAN
TAJIKISTAN
PAKISTAN
ALTAY MOUNTAINS
Lake Balkhash

N
W E
S

0   200   400   600 kilometers
0   200   400   600 miles
Conic Projection

70°E 80°E 90°E 100°E 110°E 120°E 130°E 140°E
20°N 30°N 40°N 50°N

Antarctica

Read the paragraph for background information. Then use the map to answer the questions.

Did you know? There is very little life on Antarctica. Only a few primitive plants and insects live on the ice. However, the water that surrounds it is rich in plant and animal life. All of this region south of 60°S is protected under a treaty that preserves the continent for non-military scientific purposes. Plant and animal fossils found on the continent indicate that it was not always covered in ice. At one point it supported mammals, marsupials, trees, and other plants.

1. Why aren't there any cities listed on the continent?

   _____

2. Where do the meridians meet?   _____

3. Which special line of latitude is at about 66.5°S?   _____

4. Is the greater portion of Antarctica in the Eastern Hemisphere
   or the Western Hemisphere?   _____

5. If you wanted to take a sled to the South Pole, what might be the best place to land? Explain.

   _____

6. Approximately how far is it from the southern coast of
   Roosevelt Island to the South Pole?   _____

7. What is the approximate location in latitude and longitude
   of Berkner Island?   _____

8. Which mountain range divides the continent into east and west Antarctica? How do you think it got its name?

   _____

9. Meridians are numbered from 0° to 180° and back. Only one meridian has the same measurement in the hemispheres through which it travels. The answer is not printed on the map, but there are plenty of clues. Can you identify it? _____

10. If you land at Marie Byrd Land and you take your dog sleds to the South Pole, then continue on to a waiting ship at Enderby Land, in what direction have you traveled?

    _____

Maps: The World © 2005 Creative Teaching Press

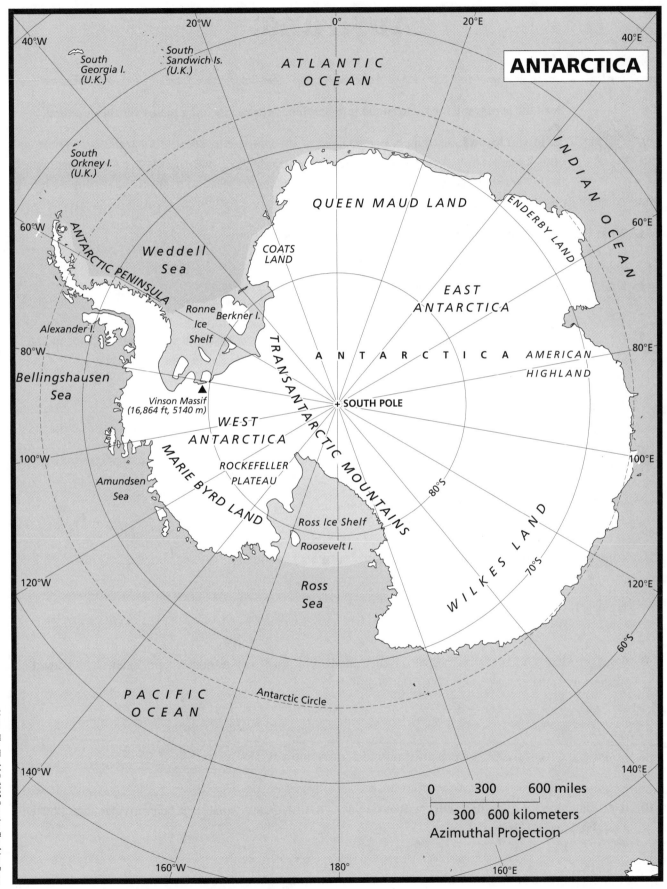

ANTARCTICA

40°W • 20°W • 0° • 20°E • 40°E

South Georgia I. (U.K.)

South Sandwich Is. (U.K.)

ATLANTIC OCEAN

INDIAN OCEAN

South Orkney I. (U.K.)

60°W

QUEEN MAUD LAND

ENDERBY LAND

60°E

ANTARCTIC PENINSULA

Weddell Sea

COATS LAND

EAST ANTARCTICA

Alexander I.

Ronne Ice Shelf

Berkner I.

TRANSANTARCTIC MOUNTAINS

80°W

ANTARCTICA

AMERICAN HIGHLAND

80°E

Bellingshausen Sea

▲ Vinson Massif (16,864 ft, 5140 m)

+ SOUTH POLE

WEST ANTARCTICA

100°W

ROCKEFELLER PLATEAU

MARIE BYRD LAND

80°S

100°E

Amundsen Sea

Ross Ice Shelf

Roosevelt I.

70°S

WILKES LAND

120°W

Ross Sea

60°S

120°E

Antarctic Circle

PACIFIC OCEAN

140°W

140°E

0   300   600 miles

0   300   600 kilometers

Azimuthal Projection

160°W • 180° • 160°E

Name_____ Date_____

Australia

N
W ⊕ **E**
S

Read the paragraph for background information. Then use the map to answer the questions.

Did you know? Australia is the smallest of the continents. Because Australia is so far from other large land masses, it has some very unique animals. It has the only egg-laying mammals in the world. Australia is the only country that does not have to share its continent with any other country. This does provide some political advantages.

1. What is the approximate location in latitude and longitude of Mount Isa?   _____

2. Which city sits exactly on the Tropic of Capricorn and is nearest to 150°E?   _____

3. You are driving through the sparsely populated Wiluna in western Australia when you realize you can only go about another 350 mi (482 km) on the gas you have left. Do you head to Geraldton or Kalgoorlie? Why?

_____

4. Which city is NE of Port Lincoln?   _____

5. What highway connects the three cities of Tasmania?   _____

6. What is the approximate distance from Mount Isa to Rockhampton?   _____

7. What is the capital city of Australia?

_____

8. Based on what you know about people and their needs, which part of Australia is more likely to be a desert: Western Australia or New South Wales? On what do you base your hypothesis?

_____

9. If you drive from Hyden to Fremantle, in which direction will you be traveling? _____

10. If driving directly to Katherine from Toowoomba, what highways would you take? Include directional abbreviations (e.g., Hwy 1N).

_____

Maps: The World © 2005 Creative Teaching Press

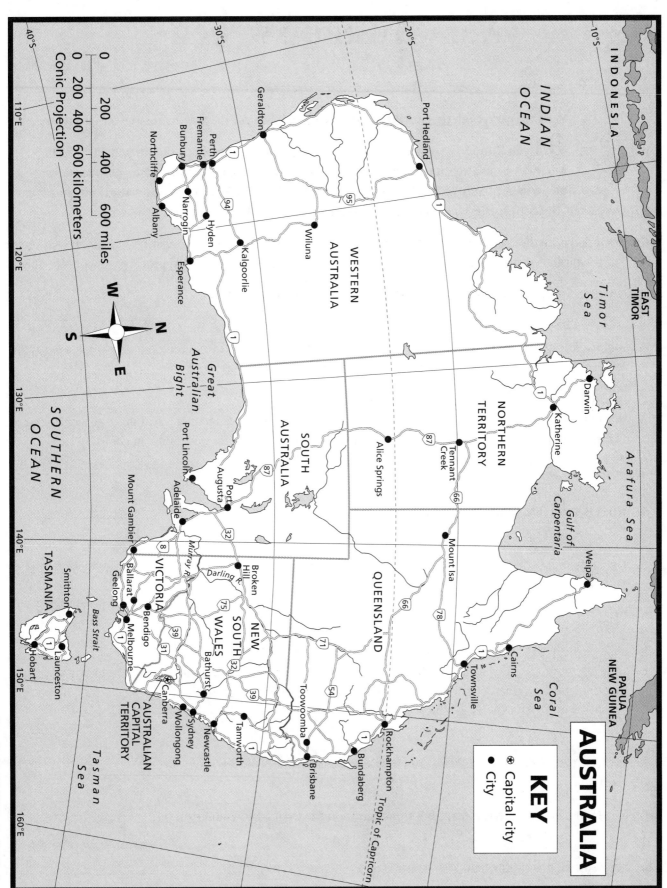

AUSTRALIA

KEY
⊗ Capital city
● City

INDONESIA

EAST TIMOR

PAPUA NEW GUINEA

INDIAN OCEAN

Timor Sea

Arafura Sea

Coral Sea

Tasman Sea

SOUTHERN OCEAN

Great Australian Bight

Gulf of Carpentaria

Bass Strait

WESTERN AUSTRALIA

NORTHERN TERRITORY

SOUTH AUSTRALIA

QUEENSLAND

NEW SOUTH WALES

VICTORIA

TASMANIA

AUSTRALIAN CAPITAL TERRITORY

Geraldton
Port Hedland
Perth
Fremantle
Bunbury
Northcliffe
Albany
Narrogin
Hyden
Esperance
Wiluna
Kalgoorlie
Darwin
Katherine
Weipa
Alice Springs
Tennant Creek
Mount Isa
Townsville
Cairns
Rockhampton
Bundaberg
Toowoomba
Brisbane
Tamworth
Newcastle
Sydney
Wollongong
Canberra
Bathurst
Broken Hill
Darling R.
Murray R.
Melbourne
Bendigo
Ballarat
Geelong
Mount Gambier
Adelaide
Port Augusta
Port Lincoln
Smithton
Launceston
Hobart

Tropic of Capricorn

10°S
20°S
30°S
40°S

110°E
120°E
130°E
140°E
150°E
160°E

0   200   400   600 kilometers
0   200   400   600 miles
Conic Projection

N S E W

Name_____ Date_____

Norway and Sweden

Read the paragraph for background information. Then use the map to answer the questions.

Did **you know?** Norway and Sweden are sometimes referred to as Scandanavia. Most of Norway's population lives in its southern half in the area around Oslo. Norway was once home to the mighty Vikings, a seafaring people who made their living by attacking and raiding the coasts of the British Isles, the coasts of western Europe, and even the interior of Russia.

Sweden is known for its political neutrality. It tries to play a balancing role in the world's politics. It was once a rural, less educated section of Europe. It now has a highly industrialized economy, provides support for the poor, and has a standard of living and life expectancy that is among the highest in the world.

1. Which city is at approximately 67.5°N and 20°E? _____

2. Approximately how far is Umea from Sundsvall? _____

3. You live in the city of Oslo and decide to get away to the coast for a summer vacation. You want to go as far north as possible, without actually crossing the Arctic Circle. Where could you go?
_____

4. What is the approximate location in latitude and longitude of Oslo? _____

5. Two other countries are sometimes considered part of Scandanavia. They are the countries closest to Norway and Sweden. Which countries are they?
_____

6. Which is closer to Oslo, Skien or Lillehammer? _____

7. Directly west of Stockholm is which city? _____

8. Through what gulf might the Vikings have accessed the interior of Russia? _____

9. In which direction are you traveling if you go from Fredrikstad to Drammen? _____

10. Umea, Sweden is on the banks of which river? _____

Maps: The World © 2005 Creative Teaching Press

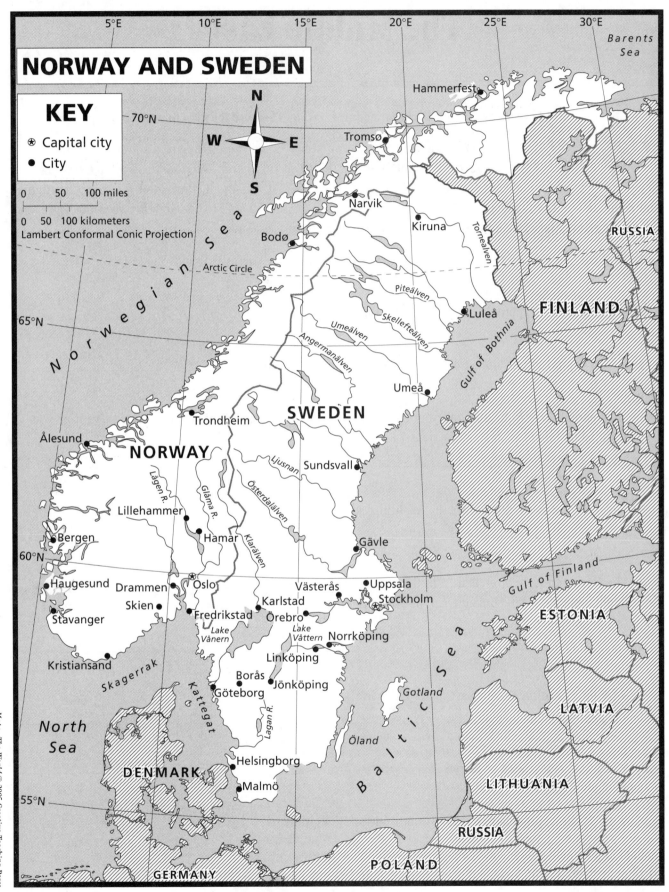

NORWAY AND SWEDEN

KEY

⊛ Capital city
● City

0   50   100 miles

0   50   100 kilometers
Lambert Conformal Conic Projection

5°E   10°E   15°E   20°E   25°E   30°E

Barents Sea

70°N

N
W   E
S

Hammerfest

Tromsø

Narvik

Bodø

Kiruna

Tornealven

Arctic Circle

65°N

Piteälven

Luleå

FINLAND

RUSSIA

Skellefteälven

Umeälven

Angermanälven

Umeå

Gulf of Bothnia

Norwegian Sea

SWEDEN

Trondheim

Ålesund

NORWAY

Ljusnan

Sundsvall

Lågen R.

Glåma R.

Österdalälven

Lillehammer

Hamar

Klarälven

Bergen

Gävle

60°N

Haugesund   Drammen   ⊛ Oslo

Västerås   Uppsala

Skien

Karlstad

Stockholm

Stavanger

Fredrikstad

Örebro

Lake Vänern

Lake Vättern

Norrköping

Kristiansand

Linköping

Skagerrak

Borås

Jönköping

Gotland

ESTONIA

Baltic Sea

LATVIA

Kattegat

Göteborg

Lagan R.

Öland

Gulf of Finland

North Sea

DENMARK

Helsingborg

Malmö

LITHUANIA

55°N

RUSSIA

GERMANY

POLAND

Maps: The World © 2005 Creative Teaching Press

Name_____ Date_____

The Middle East

Read the paragraph for background information. Then use the map to answer the questions.

Did you know? The Middle East is sometimes called the birthplace of civilization. It was the home of the Phoenicians who outgrew their Lebanon home and developed a huge trading empire along the coast of the Mediterranean Sea. It was the birthplace of Judaism, Christianity, and Islam. It was the fertile ground on which the first nomads settled, and in the area between the Tigris and Euphrates rivers, the place where the earliest preserved writing was found.

1. Find the location on the map where the earliest preserved writing was found. Shade in this area.

2. Which city is at approximately 32°N and 44°E? _____

3. Which capital city is almost directly north of Amman, Jordan? _____

4. Your parents live in Kirkuk and your spouse's parents live in Mosul. Which town do you live in if you want to be fair to both sets of parents? Explain.

   _____

5. Through which countries does the Euphrates River pass?

   _____   _____   _____

6. The fertile crescent stretched from the coast of the Mediterranean Sea to the mouths of the Tigris and Euphrates rivers. Which countries shown on the map are in the same location as the ancient world's fertile crescent?

   _____   _____   _____

7. Why do you think there aren't many cities in the Syrian Desert?

   _____

8. Which city is southeast of Beirut? _____

9. What is the approximate location in latitude and longitude of Al Basra, Iraq? _____

10. Approximately how far is it from Damascus to Dayr az Zawr? _____

Maps: *The World* © 2005 Creative Teaching Press

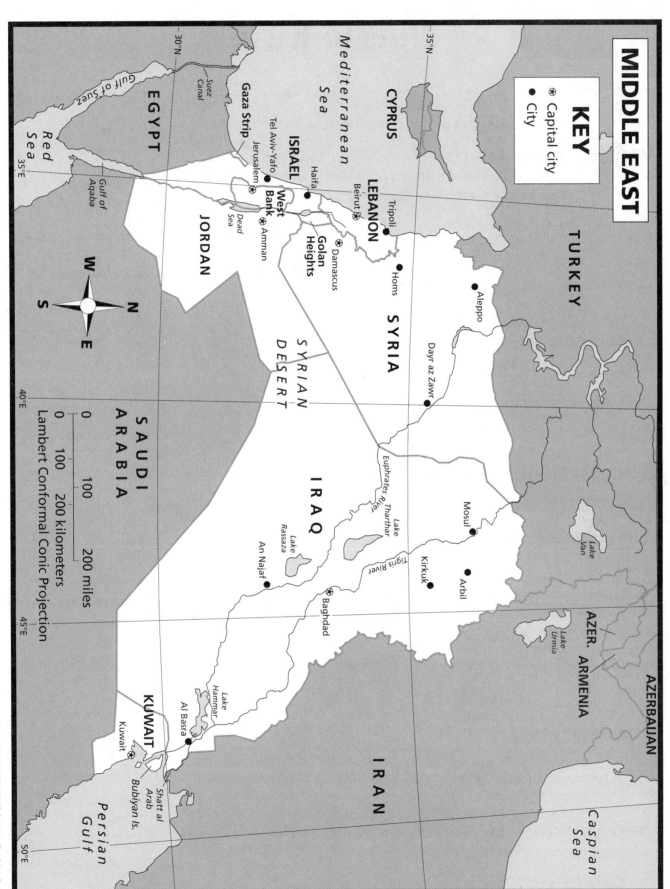

MIDDLE EAST

KEY

⊗ Capital city
● City

TURKEY

CYPRUS

Mediterranean Sea

LEBANON
Tripoli
Beirut ⊗
● Homs
● Aleppo

SYRIA

Dayr az Zawr ●

ISRAEL
Haifa ●
Tel Aviv-Yafo ●
Jerusalem ⊗
West Bank
Gaza Strip
Golan Heights
Damascus ⊗
Dead Sea

SYRIAN DESERT

JORDAN
Amman ⊗

EGYPT

Suez Canal
Gulf of Suez

Red Sea

Gulf of Aqaba

35°E

35°N

30°N

Lake Tharthar
Euphrates River

Mosul ●
Kirkuk ●
Arbil ●

Lake Van

IRAQ

Lake Rassaza
An Najaf ●
Tigris River

Baghdad ⊗

AZER.
ARMENIA
Lake Urmia

AZERBAIJAN

Caspian Sea

IRAN

SAUDI ARABIA

KUWAIT
Kuwait ⊗
Al Basra ●
Lake Hammar
Shatt al Arab
Bubiyan Is.

Persian Gulf

40°E
45°E
50°E

N
W   E
S

0   100   200 kilometers
0   100   200 miles
Lambert Conformal Conic Projection

Maps: The World © 2005 Creative Teaching Press

Puerto Rico

Read the paragraph for background information. Then use the map to answer the questions.

Did **you know?** Puerto Rico is an American territory in the Caribbean Sea. If it were to become the 51st American state, it would be the third-smallest state in the Union, larger only than Delaware and Rhode Island.

1. What is the approximate location in latitude and longitude of Manati? _____

2. What is the capital city of Puerto Rico? _____

3. Which city is directly south of Aguadilla? _____

4. Name two smaller islands associated with Puerto Rico.

   _____   _____

5. Most of the cities shown are on the edge of a _____ or the _____.

6. Which city is at approximately 18°20'N and 66°W? _____

7. Approximately how many miles across is the island from its northern shore to its southern shore? _____

8. Which city is closer to Coamo: Utuado or Caguas? _____

9. Which city is northeast of Utuado? _____

10. Which city sits exactly on 18°N? _____

Maps: The World © 2005 Creative Teaching Press

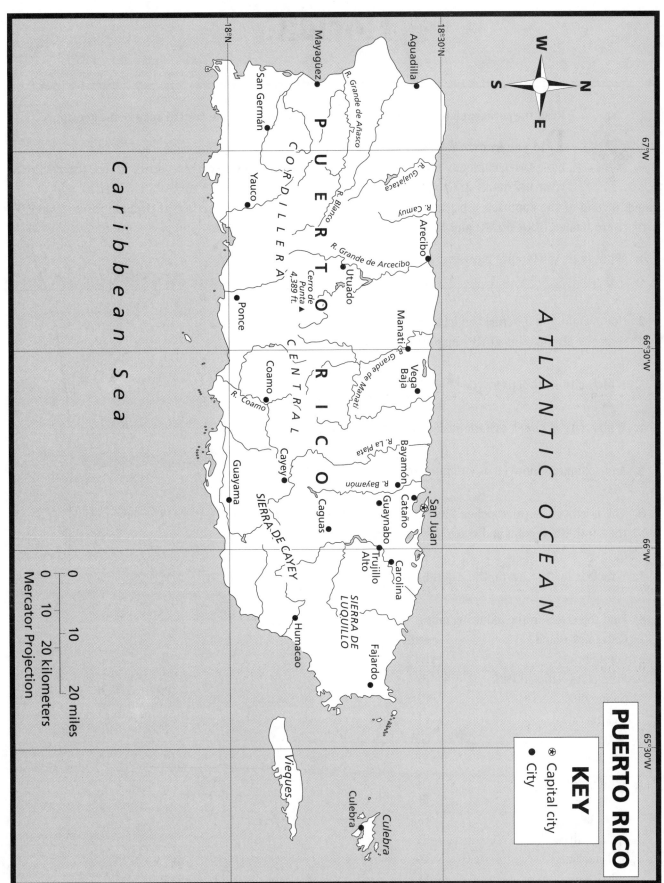

PUERTO RICO

KEY
⊕ Capital city
● City

ATLANTIC OCEAN

18°30'N

18°N

Aguadilla

Mayagüez

R. Grande de Añasco

San Germán

P U E R T O

C O R D I L L E R A

Yauco

R. Blanco

R. Guatataca

R. Camuy

Arecibo

R. Grande de Arecibo

Utuado

Cerro de
Punta ▲
4,389 ft.

Ponce

R I C O

C E N T R A L

Manatí

Vega
Baja

R. Grande de Manatí

Coamo

R. Coamo

Bayamón

R. La Plata

R. Bayamón

Cataño

Guaynabo

San Juan

Cayey

Caguas

Carolina

Trujillo
Alto

Guayama

SIERRA DE CAYEY

SIERRA DE
LUQUILLO

Fajardo

Humacao

Caribbean Sea

Vieques

Culebra

67°W

66°30'W

66°W

65°30'W

0   10   20 kilometers
0   10   20 miles
Mercator Projection

Maps: The World © 2005 Creative Teaching Press

Florida

N
W E
S

Read the paragraph for background information. Then use the map to answer the questions.

Did **you know?** You can't accuse Floridians of being too concerned about tradition. They have two completely different rivers with the same name (Withlacoochee River—the northern river originates in Georgia), a crypt in Key West is inscribed "I told you I was sick," and the names of two of the approach procedures that all aircraft follow into their arrival at Orlando International Airport are named GOOFY TWO and MINEE TWO.

1. What is the difference between ⁴¹ and ⁴⁰ ?

   _____

2. How would you describe the location of Port Charlotte to someone else looking at this map?   _____

3. Which city is directly north of Hollywood, Florida?   _____

4. Which city is closer to Tallahassee: Gainesville or Pensacola?   _____

5. Approximately how far is Orlando from Tampa?   _____

6. The northern Withlacoochee River originates in Georgia and ends when it hits the Suwannee River. Find the southern version and trace it with a crayon or marker.

7. Which is farther north, the capital city or Orlando?   _____

8. Find the errors in the following index:

Cedar Key Island	D–E2
Coral Springs	G4
Everglades National Park	F5
Gainesville	E2
Jacksonville	F1
Miami	G5
Orlando	F2
Panama City	A1
Pensacola	B1
Sarasota	E5
Spring Hill	E3
St. Petersburg	E3
Tallahassee	F1

   _____

   _____

   _____

Maps: The World © 2005 Creative Teaching Press

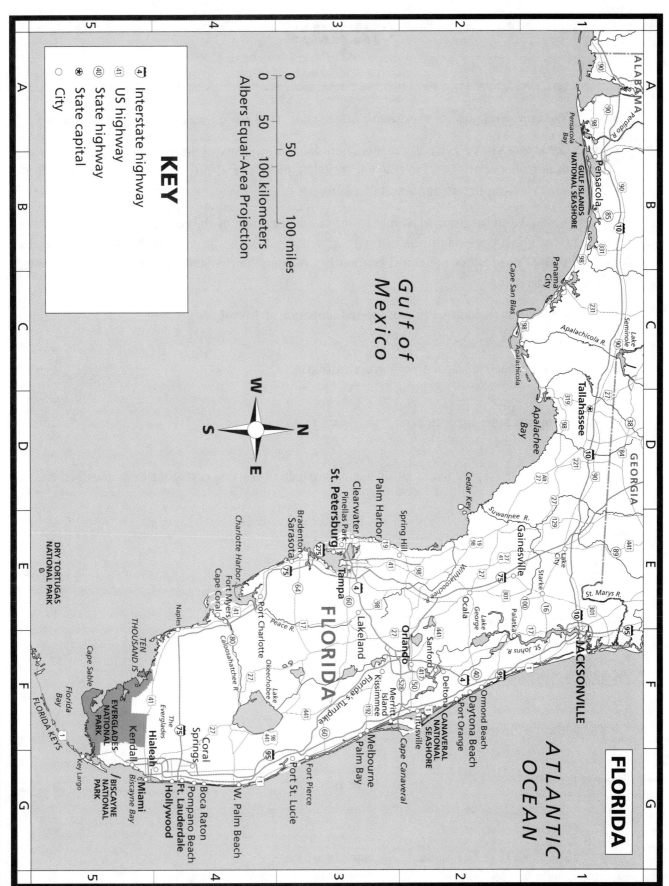

KEY

- ④ Interstate highway
- ㊽ US highway
- ㊵ State highway
- ✸ State capital
- ○ City

Albers Equal-Area Projection

0   50   100 kilometers

0   50   100 miles

FLORIDA

Gulf of Mexico

ATLANTIC OCEAN

ALABAMA

GEORGIA

N W S E

Pensacola
Pensacola Bay
Perdido R.
GULF ISLANDS NATIONAL SEASHORE
Panama City
Cape San Blas
Apalachicola
Apalachicola R.
Apalachee Bay
Lake Seminole
Tallahassee
Cedar Key
Suwannee R.
Gainesville
Lake City
Starke
Palatka
St. Marys R.
St. Johns R.
JACKSONVILLE
Ocala
Lake George
Withlacoochee
Spring Hill
Palm Harbor
Clearwater
Pinellas Park
St. Petersburg
Tampa
Bradenton
Sarasota
Charlotte Harbor
Port Charlotte
Peace R.
Fort Myers
Cape Coral
Caloosahatchee R.
Naples
Lakeland
Orlando
Kissimmee
Sanford
Deltona
Merritt Island
Titusville
CANAVERAL NATIONAL SEASHORE
Cape Canaveral
Melbourne
Palm Bay
Ormond Beach
Daytona Beach
Port Orange
FLORIDA
Florida's Turnpike
Lake Okeechobee
The Everglades
Coral Springs
Hialeah
Kendall
Miami
Biscayne Bay
BISCAYNE NATIONAL PARK
Hollywood
Ft. Lauderdale
Pompano Beach
Boca Raton
W. Palm Beach
Port St. Lucie
Fort Pierce
EVERGLADES NATIONAL PARK
Cape Sable
Florida Bay
TEN THOUSAND IS.
DRY TORTUGAS NATIONAL PARK
FLORIDA KEYS
Key Largo

A B C D E F G

1 2 3 4 5

Japan

Read the paragraph for background information. Then use the map to answer the questions.

Did you know? Japan is a mountainous land with plenty of active and dormant volcanoes. It does not have a lot of topsoil, but its mild climate and plentiful rain make it possible to grow abundant crops and sustain large forests.

Like China and Russia, Japan sought to be a superpower at the beginning of the century. Its desire to establish colonies and develop into a large empire clashed with American goals, and the two countries were at war during World War II. The United States ended that conflict by dropping the first and last atomic bombs ever used on Hiroshima and Nagasaki.

1. What is the approximate location in latitude and longitude of Tokyo? _____

2. What is the approximate distance from Nagoya to Tokyo? _____

3. Which city appears to be closer to Yamagata: Niigata or Akita?

4. What is the approximate location in latitude and longitude of the two cities that were destroyed by atomic bombs?

   _____   _____

5. Which city is northeast of Akita? _____

6. Which large island is farthest north? _____

7. Which city will you find at approximately 45°10'N and 142°E? _____

8. On which island is Tokyo located? _____

9. What two small islands are farthest south of Japan?

   _____   _____

10. If you took a plane from Kagoshima to Nagasaki, in which
    direction would you be flying? _____

Maps: The World © 2005 Creative Teaching Press

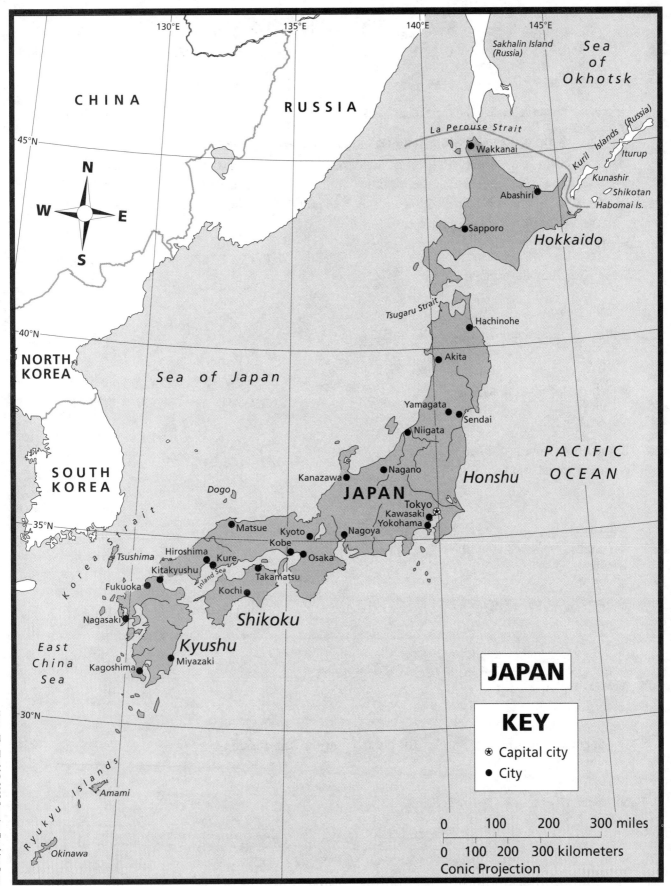

CHINA

RUSSIA

Sakhalin Island
(Russia)

Sea
of
Okhotsk

La Perouse Strait

Kuril Islands (Russia)

Iturup

Kunashir

Shikotan

Habomai Is.

Wakkanai

Abashiri

Sapporo

Hokkaido

45°N

130°E   135°E   140°E   145°E

N
W   E
S

NORTH
KOREA

Sea of Japan

Tsugaru Strait

Hachinohe

Akita

40°N

SOUTH
KOREA

Dogo

Yamagata

Sendai

Niigata

Honshu

PACIFIC
OCEAN

Kanazawa   Nagano

JAPAN

35°N

Korea Strait

Matsue

Kyoto

Tokyo

Kawasaki
Yokohama

Tsushima

Hiroshima

Kobe

Nagoya

Kure

Inland Sea

Osaka

Kitakyushu

Takamatsu

Fukuoka

Kochi

Shikoku

Nagasaki

Kyushu

East
China
Sea

Kagoshima   Miyazaki

30°N

Ryukyu Islands

Amami

Okinawa

JAPAN

KEY

⊛ Capital city

● City

0   100   200   300 miles

0   100 200 300 kilometers

Conic Projection

Western Russia

Read the paragraph for background information. Then use the map to answer the questions.

Did you know? Historically, the city of St. Petersburg was very important. In fact, at one point it was the capital city of Russia. From St. Petersburg, the Russians could sail through the Baltic Sea and out into the Atlantic Ocean. From there they could trade along the coast of Western Africa. Because of its location, St. Petersburg was prone to flooding. Modern St. Petersburg has a system of dikes and canals to control the flood waters. Today, St. Petersburg is a popular place for tourists to visit because of the beautiful buildings and canals.

1. What river runs through Saratov? _____

2. Which city is at approximately 40°N and 33°E? _____

3. Which city is south of Saransk (54°30'N, ˜45°E)? _____

4. If you drove from Astrakhan to Rostov, in what general direction would you be driving? _____

5. What is the approximate location in latitude and longitude of the city that is separated from the rest of the country? _____

6. Which two port towns are closer together: Archangel and Mezen or Pechenga and Murmansk?

   _____   _____

7. How far is Kotlas from Konosha? _____

8. Which city on the banks of the Volga River is also near the Caspian Sea? _____

9. Name the river that passes by Pechora. _____

10. What city lays along the Volga River at about 56°30'N and 35°30'E? _____

Maps: The World © 2005 Creative Teaching Press

WESTERN RUSSIA

KEY
⊛ Capital city
● City

10°E   20°E   30°E   40°E   50°E   60°E   70°E

70°N

Kara Sea

Barents Sea

● Amderma

Pechenga ●
Murmansk ●

● Naryan Mar   ● Salekhard

Pechora R.

Mezen ●   ● Pechora   *Ob R.*

White Sea

Belomorsk ●   ● Archangel

S W E D E N

Gulf of Bothnia

F I N L A N D

Northern Dvina R.   *Vychegda R.*

60°N

Lake Ladoga   *Lake Onega*

Konosha ●   ● Kotlas   ● Syktyvkar

Helsinki ⊛   ● Vyborg

Stockholm ⊛   *Gulf of Finland*

R U S S I A

● Berezniki

Tallinn ⊛   St. Petersburg ●   ● Nizhniy Tagil

ESTONIA   *Lake Peipus*   ● Vologda   ● Perm   ● Yekaterinburg

● Novgorod   *Rybinsk Reservoir*   Kirov ●

Riga ⊛   ● Pskov   Izhevsk ●   ● Chelyabinsk

LATVIA   Tver ●   *Volga R.*   Yaroslavl ●   *Kama R.*

LITHUANIA   *Dvina R.*   Nizhniy   Kazan ●   ● Ufa

Kaliningrad ●   ⊛ Vilnius   Moscow ⊛   *Oka R.*   Novgorod ●   ● Magnitogorsk

Minsk ⊛   Ulyanovsk ●

Warsaw ⊛   **B E L A R U S**   Smolensk ●   *Oka R.*   Tula ●   ● Togliatti

P O L A N D   Bryansk ●   Saransk ●   ● Samara

50°N   Penza ●   Kuznetsk ●   Orenburg ●

Bug R.   *Desna R.*   ● Orel   Tambov ●   *Ural R.*

SLOVAKIA   **U K R A I N E**   Kursk ●   Voronezh ●   **K A Z A K H S T A N**

⊛ Kiev   *Dnieper R.*   *Don R.*   Saratov ●

Budapest ⊛   *Dniester R.*   *Donets R.*   *Volga R.*

HUNGARY   **MOLDAVIA**   Chisinau ●   Volgograd ●

R O M A N I A   *Pruf R.*

Belgrade ●   Rostov ●   Astrakhan ●   N

SERBIA-   *Sea of Azov*   *Caspian Sea*   W   E

MONTENEGRO   Bucharest ●   Krasnodar ●   S

Danube R.   Armavir ●

⊛ Sofia   **BULGARIA**   Groznyy ●   **UZBEKISTAN**

⊛ Skopje   *Black Sea*

GREECE   **GEORGIA**

40°N   Tbilisi ⊛   Baku ●

TURKEY   **ARMENIA**   **AZERBAIJAN**   **TURKMENISTAN**

Ankara ⊛   Yerevan ●

● Athens   0   200   400 miles   **AZERBAIJAN**

0   200   400 kilometers

Lambert Conformal Conic Projection

I R A N

Maps: The World © 2005 Creative Teaching Press

Western Russia   35

India

Read the paragraph for background information. Then use the map to answer the questions.

Did you know? India began along the banks of the Ganges River as one of the four major river civilizations of the ancient world. It has a long and rich history as an empire, a religious people, and a successful people. India ranks right behind China in world population, although it is a much smaller country. It is one of the most ethnically diverse populations in the world, and although great strides have been made to even out the opportunities for all of its people, violence still occasionally erupts between groups.

1. India disagrees with Afghanistan and China about exactly where its borders are. What symbol is shown on the map to show the area that is in question? _____

2. Which two cities shown on the map sit on or touch the Tropic of Cancer?

   _____   _____

3. Which city will you find at 26°N and 92°E? _____

4. Which city is southwest of Vishakhapatnam? _____

5. What is the distance from Indore to Varanasi? _____

6. What is the approximate location in latitude and longitude of Jabalpur? _____

7. Find the river on which the ancient river civilization was built. Trace that river with a crayon or marker.

8. Which city is directly south of Pune?

   _____

9. You start in Bangladore and fly straight north to Bhopal. What rivers do you fly over on your way?

   _____   _____   _____   _____

10. What is the distance from Pune to Vadodara?

   _____

Maps: The World © 2005 Creative Teaching Press

KEY
✴ Capital city
● City

TAJIKISTAN

AFGHANISTAN

Disputed border

Disputed borders

KASHMIR

Indus R.

● Srinagar

CHINA

HIMALAYAS

30°N

PAKISTAN

● Amritsar
● Jullundur

● Ludhiana
● Chandigarh

GREAT INDIAN (THAR) DESERT

● Delhi ● Meerut
New Delhi ✴
● Aligarh

● Agra

● Jaipur

● Jodhpur

Chambal R.

● Gwalior

Yamuna R.

● Bareilly

● Lucknow

● Kanpur ● Gorakhpur

● Allahabad

● Varanasi

NEPAL

Ganga (Ganges) R.

● Patna

BHUTAN

Brahmaputra R.

● Gauhati

BANGLADESH

INDIA

● Ahmādabad

● Bhopal

● Indore

● Vadodara

● Rajkot

Narmada R.

● Jabalpur

Tapti R.

● Surat

● Nasik

● Nagpur

● Ranchi

● Jamshedpur

Mahanadi R.

● Haora

● Kolkata (Calcutta)

Tropic of Cancer

MYANMAR (BURMA)

20°N

Thane ●
● Kalyan

Mumbai (Bombay) ●

● Aurangabad

● Pune

● Sholapur

DECCAN PLATEAU

EASTERN GHATS

Godavari R.

Krishna R.

● Hyderabad

WESTERN GHATS

● Goa
● Hubli

Penner R.

Guntur ●

● Vishakhapatnam

Bay of Bengal

● Vijayawada

Arabian Sea

● Bangalore

● Mysore

● Chennai (Madras)

N
W   E
S

Andaman Is.

Andaman Sea

Lakshadweep

● Coimbatore

10°N

Laccadive Sea

● Cochin
● Madurai

● Trivandrum

Gulf of Mannar

SRI LANKA

Nicobar Is.

MALDIVES

INDIAN OCEAN

| 0 | 200 | 400 | 600 miles |

| 0 | 200 | 400 | 600 kilometers |

Conic Projection

INDONESIA

70°E

80°E

90°E

Central Europe

Read the paragraph for background information. Then use the map to answer the questions.

Did you know? Poland is largely Roman Catholic and the election of the current Pope, the first Polish Pope, was very encouraging to the Polish people. It seemed a sign of better times to come.

The Czech Republic and Slovakia were briefly a single country, but once they achieved independence they reverted to being separate countries. Hungary has the largest freshwater lake—Lake Balatan—in Europe.

Romania has a reputation for the most accomplished gymnasts at the Olympics. This is an area with a rich history and a very active present.

1. Which capital city is at approximately 45°N and 20°E? _____

2. Which countries fall along the southwestern side of the Carpathian Mountains?

   _____   _____   _____

3. What is the approximate distance from Poznan to Lodz? _____

4. What is the approximate location of the largest freshwater lake in Europe? What is the name of this lake?

   _____

5. Which city is northwest of Bucharest, Romania? _____

6. Which river is part of the boundary between Slovakia and Hungary? _____

7. What is the approximate location in latitude and longitude of Krakow, Poland? _____

8. Which neighboring capital city is closest to Sofia, Bulgaria? _____

9. Which city is southeast of Novi Sad, Serbia-Montenegro? _____

10. Which three cities line the coast of the Black Sea?

    _____   _____   _____

Maps: The World © 2005 Creative Teaching Press

Baltic Sea

LITHUANIA

RUSSIA

CENTRAL EUROPE

Gdansk

NORTH EUROPEAN PLAIN

BELARUS

KEY

Szczecin

⊛ Capital city

● City

GERMANY

Poznan

POLAND

⊛ Warsaw

Lodz

Lublin

0   50   100   150 miles

Wroclaw

Oder R.

Czestochowa

Vistula R.

0   50 100 150 kilometers

Katowice

Krakow

Lambert Conformal Conic Projection

50°N

CZECH REP.

UKRAINE

N

SLOVAKIA

Kosice

CARPATHIAN MOUNTAINS

W   E

Bratislava

Danube R.

S

MOLDOVA

AUSTRIA

Budapest

Debrecen

Iasi

HUNGARY

Cluj-Napoca

HUNGARIAN PLAIN

ROMANIA

Brasov

Galati

SLOVENIA

Ljubljana

⊛ Zagreb

CROATIA

Rijeka

TRANSYLVANIAN ALPS

45°N

Novi Sad

BOSNIA & HERZEGOVINA

Belgrade

Bucharest

Constanta

DINARIC ALPS

Craiova

Danube R.

Split

Sarajevo

SERBIA-MONTENEGRO

Varna

Mostar

BALKAN MOUNTAINS

Burgas

Black Sea

Adriatic Sea

Pristina

⊛ Sofia

BULGARIA

Plovdiv

⊛ Skopje

MACEDONIA

TURKEY

ITALY

ALBANIA

GREECE

40°N 15°E

20°E

25°E

Name_____ Date_____

West Africa

Read the paragraph for background information. Then use the map to answer the questions.

Did you know? Much of West Africa was a French colony in the early part of this century. Senegal, Guinea, Burkina Faso, Cote D'Ivoire, and Mali were French. Consequently, French is the dominant language in these countries. Ghana, Sierra Leone, and Gambia were British territories.

Africa struggles more with health issues compared to the rest of the world. It is the country hardest hit by AIDS, where it continues to take more lives each year. Even so, countries like Senegal provide excellent examples of what can be accomplished in improving the health of its people with effort and education.

1. In West Africa, where are most of the capital cities located?

   a. in the water
   b. along the coast
   c. in the desert
   d. in the mountains

2. Which English-speaking country is between 10˚W and 20˚W?

   a. Guinea
   b. Cote D'Ivoire
   c. Sierra Leone
   d. Burkina Faso

3. Which capital city is at approximately 5˚N and 0˚?

   a. Accra, Ghana
   b. Ouagadougou, Burkina Faso
   c. Cotonou, Togo
   d. Conakry, Guinea

4. What is the approximate distance from Abidjan, Cote D'Ivoire to Sekondi-Takordi, Ghana?

   a. ˜210 mi or ˜320 km
   b. ˜320 mi or ˜210 km
   c. ˜600 mi or ˜600 km
   d. ˜200 mi or ˜300 km

5. What is the approximate location in latitude and longitude of Timbuktu, Mali?

   a. 3˚N, 17˚W
   b. 17˚S, 3˚W
   c. 20˚N, 13˚W
   d. 17˚N, 3˚W

6. Which city is southwest of Marrakech, Morocco?

   a. Casablanca, Morocco
   b. Rabat, Morocco
   c. Constantine, Algeria
   d. Laayoune, Western Sahara

Maps The World © 2005 Creative Teaching Press

WEST AFRICA

KEY

⊛ Capital city
● City

ATLANTIC OCEAN

20°W 10°W 0° 10°E

PORTUGAL
SPAIN
Mediterranean Sea

Algiers ●
Tunis ●

Strait of Gibraltar
Ceuta (SPAIN)
Tangier ●
Melilla (SPAIN)
Oran ●
Constantine ●

⊛ Rabat
Casablanca ●

MOROCCO *ATLAS MOUNTAINS*

TUNISIA

● Marrakech

30°N

ALGERIA

S A H A R A

LIBYA

Canary Islands (SPAIN)

● Laayoune

Western Sahara (MOROCCO)

AHAGGAR MOUNTAINS

20°N

MAURITANIA

MALI

NIGER

⊛ Nouakchott

Timbuktu ● *Niger R.*

⊛ Dakar **SENEGAL**
GAMBIA
Banjul ●
Gambia R.
Bissau ●

● Bamako

BURKINA FASO

Ouagadougou ●

White Volta R.
Black Volta R.

GUINEA-BISSAU

GUINEA

NIGERIA

BENIN

10°N

Conakry ●

SIERRA LEONE
Freetown ⊛

CÔTE D'IVOIRE

L. Volta

GHANA

TOGO

Benue R.

Cotonou ●

LIBERIA

Yamoussoukro ⊛

Kumasi ●

Lomé ●
Porto-Novo ●

Monrovia ●

Abidjan ●

Accra ⊛

CAMEROON

Sekondi-Takordi ●

N

W   E

S

0   200   400   600 miles

0   200   400   600 kilometers

Lambert Azimuthal Equal-Area Projection

Gulf of Guinea

EQUATORIAL GUINEA

SÃO TOMÉ AND PRÍNCIPE

GABON

Indonesia

Read the paragraph for background information. Then use the map to answer the questions.

Did you know? Indonesia is the largest country in Southeast Asia. It is made up of 13,670 islands, of which more than 7,000 are uninhabited. Most of Indonesia's area is included in the three largest islands.

The people of the islands are so diverse that the only thing you can really say they have in common is that they are vulnerable to frequent earthquakes and volcanic eruptions and that they share a moist, tropical climate.

Mount Merapi erupts frequently and often destroys roads, fields, and villages. Still, it produces a rich, fertile soil that permits crops to grow well at other times. Mount Kelut is very dangerous because the water in its large crater lake is thrown out during each eruption, causing great mudflows that rush down into the flat areas of the island and destroy all before them.

1. What kind of mountain is at approximately 8°S and 112°E?

    a. hill
    b. burial mound
    c. volcano
    d. mountain range

2. Which city is located at the equator and approximately 109°30'E?

    a. Pontianak
    b. Samarinda
    c. Waigeo
    d. Padang

3. Which island is located northwest of the Island Buru?

    a. Jambie
    b. Ob
    c. Sula
    d. Ceram

4. On which island is the capital of Indonesia located?

    a. Jakarta
    b. Borneo
    c. Sumatra
    d. Java

5. What is the distance from Sorong to Ambon?

    a. ~600 mi or ~650 km
    b. ~300 mi or ~480 km
    c. ~480 km or ~600 m
    d. ~200 mi or ~310 km

6. What is the approximate location in latitude and longitude of Kupang?

    a. 10°N, 124°W
    b. 10°S, 124°E
    c. 100°S, 124°E
    d. 124°S, 110°E

Maps: The World © 2005 Creative Teaching Press

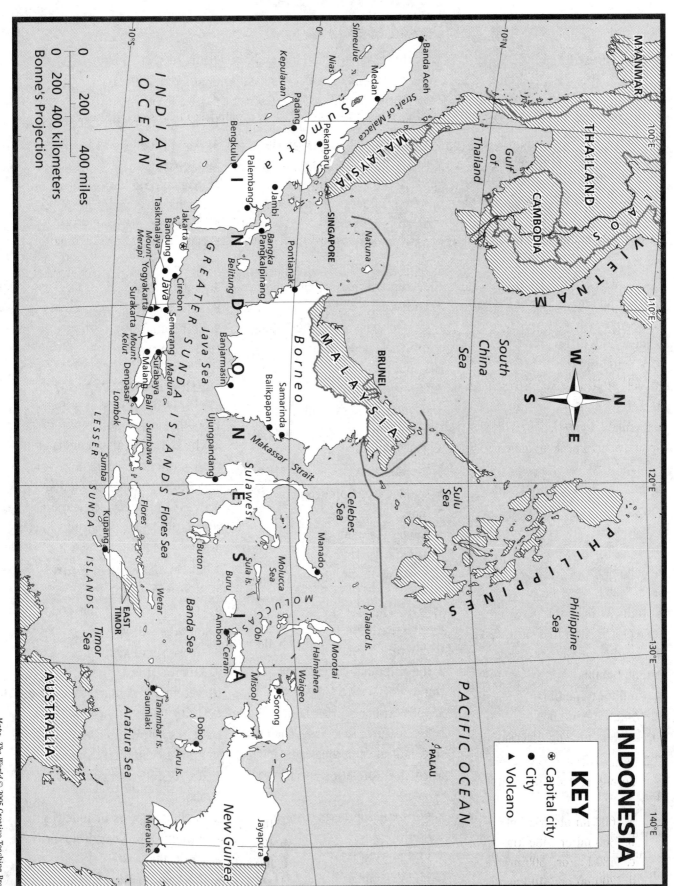

INDONESIA

KEY
⊛ Capital city
● City
▲ Volcano

MYANMAR

THAILAND

CAMBODIA

VIETNAM

Gulf of Thailand

South China Sea

PHILIPPINES

Philippine Sea

PACIFIC OCEAN

PALAU

Sulu Sea

Celebes Sea

BRUNEI

MALAYSIA

Borneo

Samarinda
Balikpapan

Sulawesi

Makassar Strait

Ujungpandang

Manado

Buton

Flores

Flores Sea

Banda Sea

Molucca Sea

MOLUCCA ISLANDS

Sula Is.
Buru
Obi
Ceram
Ambon
Misool
Halmahera
Morotai
Waigeo
Talaud Is.

Sorong

Dobo
Aru Is.
Tanimbar Is.
Saumlaki

New Guinea

Jayapura
Merauke

Arafura Sea

Timor Sea

EAST TIMOR
Wetar

LESSER SUNDA ISLANDS

Sumba
Sumbawa
Lombok
Kupang
Sumba

AUSTRALIA

INDIAN OCEAN

Simeulue
Nias
Kepulauan
Padang
Bengkulu
Palembang
Jambi

Medan
Banda Aceh
Strait of Malacca
Pekanbaru
SINGAPORE
MALAYSIA

Sumatra

INDONESIA

Bangka
Pangkalpinang
Belitung

Pontianak

Natuna

Jakarta ⊛
Bandung
Tasikmalaya
Cirebon
Mount Merapi
Yogyakarta
Surakarta
Mount Kelut
Malang
Surabaya
Semarang
Madura
Java
GREATER SUNDA ISLANDS
Java Sea
Banjarmasin
Bali
Denpasar

SINGAPORE

N W S E

Scale:
0   200   400 kilometers
0   200   400 miles
Bonne's Projection

Answer Key

Africa (Page 9)
Evaluate the Map
1. Africa
2. the countries and capitals of the continent of Africa
3. political boundaries, land and water features, key, scale, compass rose, latitude and longitude, towns or cities
4. northern, southern, eastern, western
5. 20°S to 45°N; 10°W to 50°E
6. 11/16":500 mi or 11 mm:500 km
7. answers will vary
8. answers will vary
9. Atlantic Ocean
10. accept all reasonable responses
Activity Page
1. Kampala, Uganda; Libreville, Gabon; Sao Tome, Sao Tome and Principe
2. the Blue Nile and the White Nile rivers
3. It is one of the world's largest rivers.
4. Bujumbura
5. ~15°S, 28°E
6. Addis Ababa, Ethiopia
7. Freetown, Sierra Leone; Conakry, Guinea; Bissau, Guinea-Bissau; Banjul, Gambia
8. Windhoek, Namibia
9. ~850 mi, ~1350 km
10. Answers include Algeria and Libya

Asia (Page 11)
Evaluate the Map
1. Asia
2. the countries and capitals of the continent of Asia
3. political boundaries, land and water features, key, scale, compass rose, latitude and longitude, towns or cities
4. northern, southern, eastern, western
5. 10°S to 80°N; 10°W to 170°W
6. 9/16": 500 mi or 9 mm:500 km
7. answers will vary
8. answers will vary
9. Pacific Ocean
10. accept all reasonable responses
Activity Page
1. No. The symbol for Hong Kong is a dot. The symbol for a capital city is a star.
2. Europe and Africa
3. Country names are in all caps. Island names are in regular type.
4. The Aral Sea
5. 7°N, 80°E
6. Ulananbaatar, Mongolia
7. India
8. Hanoi, Vietnam
9. Ankara, Turkey
10. ~800 mi, ~1300 km

Mexico (Page 13)
Evaluate the Map
1. Mexico
2. the cities and ruins of the country of Mexico
3. political boundaries, land and water features, key, scale, compass rose, latitude and longitude, towns or cities, information specific to people
4. northern, southern, eastern, western
5. 10°N to 33°N; 115°W to 85°W
6. 15/16":200 mi or 15 mm:200 km
7. answers will vary
8. answers will vary
9. Pacific Ocean
10. accept all reasonable responses
Activity Page
1. Mazatlán
2. ~320 mi, ~515 km
3. Mexico City
4. southwest
5. Gulf of Mexico
6. southeast
7. Chichén Itzá
8. 16°N, 100°W
9. Chihuahua
10. Pacific Ocean

South America (Page 15)
Evaluate the Map
1. South America
2. The countries and capitals of the continent of South America
3. political boundaries, land and water features, key, scale, compass rose, latitude and longitude, towns or cities
4. northern, southern, western
5. 18°N to 55°S; 30°W to 90°W
6. 13/16":500 mi or 13 mm:500 km
7. answers will vary
8. answers will vary
9. Atlantic Ocean
10. accept all reasonable responses
Activity Page
1. No, it's not. It has a city symbol and not a capital city symbol.
2. Yes, it is. It has a capital city symbol.
3. Possible answers include Negro R., Putumayo R., Ucayali R., Jurua R., and Madeira R.
4. the Amazon Basin

5. Tropic of Capricorn

6. because the bottom portion is closer to the South Pole where the lines come together

7. 19.5°S, 64.5°W

8. Quito, Ecuador

9. Recife, Brazil

10. ~250, mi, ~400 km

Europe (Page 17)
Evaluate the Map

1. Europe

2. the countries and capitals of the continent of Europe

3. political boundaries, land and water features, key, scale, compass rose, latitude and longitude, towns or cities

4. northern, eastern, western

5. 35°N to 70°N; 30°W to 60°E

6. 9/16":200 mi or 9 mm:200 km

7. answers will vary

8. answers will vary

9. Atlantic Ocean

10. accept all reasonable responses

Activity Page

1. northern Africa

2. it had access to plenty of water

3. 60°N, 30°E

4. Prague, Czech Republic

5. Portugal and Spain

6. The Baltic Sea

7. northwest

8. ~300 mi, ~480 km

9. Sarajevo, Bosnia

10. Sweden and Finland

China (Page 19)
Evaluate the Map

1. China

2. the cities and capital of the country of China

3. political boundaries, land and water features, key, scale, compass rose, latitude and longitude, towns

or cities, information specific to people (roads)

4. northern, eastern

5. 15°N to 55°N; 70°E to 140°E

6. 1/2":200 mi or 8 mm:200 km

7. answers will vary

8. answers will vary

9. East China Sea

10. accept all reasonable responses

Activity Page

1. The Tropic of Cancer

2. Lanzhou

3. Hong Kong; the English name is in parentheses.

4. It is sparsely populated. Fewer people live and work there.

5. ~230 mi, ~370 km

6. Taiyuan

7. 30°N, 120°E

8. Hailar; probably not because there are thousands of cities and not all of them are shown

9. Zhangjiang

10. Dalian

Antarctica (Page 21)
Evaluate the Map

1. Antarctica

2. the features of the continent of Antarctica

3. land and water features, scale, latitude and longitude

4. southern, eastern, western

5. 40° to 90°S; 0° to 180°W

6. 5/8":300 mi or 9 mm:300 km

7. answers will vary

8. answers will vary

9. Pacific Ocean

10. accept all reasonable responses

Activity Page

1. they don't exist

2. at the South Pole

3. Antarctic Circle

4. the Eastern Hemisphere

5. Accept all reasonable and supported answers. Previous explorers landed on the Ross Ice Shelf because this location is flat and closest to the pole.

6. ~725 mi, ~1170 km

7. 80°S, 50°W

8. Transantarctic Mountains; it goes across the continent at that point

9. 90°E becomes 90°W

10. you walked south and then north

Australia (Page 23)
Evaluate the Map

1. Australia

2. the cities and capital of the continent of Australia

3. political boundaries, land and water features, key, scale, compass rose, latitude and longitude, towns or cities, information specific to people (roads)

4. southern, eastern

5. 10°S to 40°S; 110°E to 160°E

6. 9/16":200 mi or 9 mm:200 km

7. answers will vary

8. answers will vary

9. Southern Ocean

10. accept all reasonable responses

Activity Page

1. 20.5°S, 139.5°E

2. Rockhampton

3. Kalgoorlie. It is ~300 mi (480 km) away. Geraldton is nearly 400 mi (640 km) away, and even further by highway.

4. Port Augusta

5. Highway 1

6. ~740 mi, ~1200 km

7. Canberra

8. Western Australia because it has many fewer roads and cities. Part

of it appears to be largely
unsettled.
9. west
10. 54W to 71N to 66W to 87N

Norway and Sweden (Page 25)
Evaluate the Map
1. Norway and Sweden
2. the cities and capitals of the
countries of Norway and Sweden
3. political boundaries, land and
water features, key, scale, compass
rose, latitude and longitude, towns
or cities
4. northern, eastern
5. 53°N to 75°N; 5°E to 30°E
6. 3/8":50 mi or 6 mm:50 km
7. answers will vary
8. answers will vary
9. Norwegian Sea
10. accept all reasonable responses
Activity Page
1. Kiruna, Sweden
2. ~135 mi, ~220 km
3. Trondheim in Norway, or Lulea
in Sweden
4. 60°N, 11°E
5. Denmark and Finland
6. Skien
7. Karlstad you may also accept
Orebro
8. the Gulf of Finland
(Teacher note: If students are chal-
lenged by this question, you might
wish to provide students with the
map of Western Russia on page 35.)
9. northwest
10. Umealven

The Middle East (Page 27)
Evaluate the Map
1. Middle East
2. the cities and capitals of the
countries of the Middle East
3. political boundaries, land and
water features, key, scale, compass
rose, latitude and longitude, towns
or cities
4. northern, eastern
5. 27° to 40°N; 32°E to 50°E
6. 3/4":100 mi or 12 mm:100 km
7. answers will vary
8. answers will vary
9. Mediterranean Sea
10. accept all reasonable responses
Activity Page
1. Students should shade in the
area between the Tigris and
Euphrates rivers.
2. An Najaf, Iraq
3. Beirut, Lebanon
4. Arbil, because it is equal
distance from both
5. Iraq, Syria, and Turkey
6. Syria, Lebanon, and Iraq
(although you may accept Jordan
and Israel)
7. Possible answers include that it
doesn't have enough water to grow
crops to support a large population
8. Damascus, Syria
9. 30.5°N, 48°E
10. ~250 mi, ~400 km

Puerto Rico (Page 29)
Evaluate the Map
1. Puerto Rico
2. the cities of the island of
Puerto Rico
3. land and water features, key,
scale, compass rose, latitude and
longitude, towns or cities
4. northern, western
5. 17°30'N to 19°N; 65°15'W to 67°15'W
6. 5/8":10 mi or 1 cm:10 km
7. answers will vary
8. answers will vary
9. Atlantic Ocean
10. accept all reasonable responses

Activity Page
1. 18°25'N, 66°30'W; The scale of this
map is quite small. Students may
need to review the concept of
minutes and seconds to understand
the meridian lines on this map.
2. San Juan
3. Mayaguez
4. Culebra and Vieques
5. river; ocean
6. Trujillo Alto
7. Accept all reasonable responses
of ~35 mi or ~55 km. At its widest
point it is closer to ~38 mi or
~61 km.
8. Caguas
9. Manati
10. Guayama

Florida (Page 31)
Evaluate the Map
1. Florida
2. the Key cities, rivers, and roads
of the state of Florida
3. political boundaries, land and
water features, key, scale, compass
rose, grid lines, towns or cities,
information specific to people
4. northern, western
5. N/A
6. 3/4":50 mi or 12 mm:50 km
7. answers will vary
8. answers will vary
9. Gulf of Mexico
10. accept all reasonable responses
Activity Page
1. The first is a state highway and
the second is a national highway.
2. E4
3. Ft. Lauderdale
4. Gainesville
5. ~170 mi, ~125 km
6. Students should trace the river
in E2-E3.

7. the capital city of Tallahassee

8. Panama City: C1;Tallahassee: D1; Sarasota: E3

Japan (Page 33)
Evaluate the Map

1. Japan

2. The cities and natural features of the islands of Japan

3. political boundaries, land and water features, key, scale, compass rose, latitude and longitude, towns or cities

4. northern, eastern

5. 26°N to 47°N; 127°E to 147°E

6. 9/16":100 mi or 9 mm:100 km

7. answers will vary

8. answers will vary

9. Pacific Ocean

10. accept all reasonable responses

Activity Page

1. 35°30'N, 140°E

2. ~180 mi, ~300 km

3. Niigata

4. Hiroshima: ~34°30'N, 132°30'E; Nagasaki: 33°N, 130°E

5. Hachinohe

6. Hokkaido

7. Wakkanai

8. Honshu

9. Okinawa and Amami

10. northwest

Western Russia (Page 35)
Evaluate the Map

1. Western Russia

2. the cities and capital of the western portion of Russia

3. political boundaries, land and water features, key, scale, compass rose, latitude and longitude, towns or cities

4. northern, eastern

5. 38°N to 70°N; 10°E to 70°E

6. 11/16":200 mi or 11 mm:200 km

7. answers will vary

8. answers will vary

9. Barents Sea

10. accept all reasonable responses

Activity Page

1. The Volga River

2. Ankara

3. Penza

4. west

5. Kaliningrad is at approximately 55°N, 20°E

6. Pechenga and Murmansk

7. ~235 mi, ~380 km

8. Astrakhan

9. Pechora River

10. Tver

India (Page 37)
Evaluate the Map

1. India

2. the cities and capital of the country of India

3. political boundaries, land and water features, key, scale, compass rose, latitude and longitude, towns or cities

4. northern, eastern

5. 4°N to 38°N; 70°E to 95°E

6. 11/16":200 mi or 11 mm:200 km

7. answers will vary

8. answers will vary

9. Bay of Bengal

10. accept all reasonable responses

Activity Page

1. a dashed line

2. Ranchi, and Bhopal

3. Gauhati

4. Vijayawada

5. ~370 mi, ~600 km

6. 23°N, 80°E

7. Students should trace the Ganga (Ganges) River.

8. Goa

9. Penner, Krishna, Godavari, Tapti, and Narmada

10. ~260 mi, ~420 km

Central Europe (Page 39)
Evaluate the Map

1. Central Europe

2. the capitals and countries of the central European region

3. political boundaries, land and water features, key, scale, compass rose, latitude and longitude, towns or cities

4. northern, eastern

5. 45°N to 55°N; 14°E to 30°E

6. 7/16":50 mi or 7 mm:50 km

7. answers will vary

8. answers will vary

9. Adriatic Sea

10. accept all reasonable responses

Activity Page

1. Belgrade, Serbia-Montenegro

2. Slovakia, Hungary, and Romania

3. ~130 mi, ~210 km

4. 47°N, 18°E; Lake Balatan

5. Cluj-Napoca, Romania

6. the Danube

7. 50°N, 20°E

8. Skopje, Macedonia

9. Belgrade

10. Burgas and Varna of Bulgaria and Constanta of Romania

West Africa (Page 41)
Evaluate the Map

1. West Africa

2. the capitals and countries of the west African region

3. political boundaries, land and water features, key, scale, compass rose, latitude and longitude, towns or cities

4. northern, eastern, western

5. 1° to 38°N; 20°W to 9°E

6. 11/16": 200 mi or 11 mm : 200 km

7. answers will vary

8. answers will vary

9. Atlantic Ocean

10. accept all reasonable responses

Activity Page

1. b

2. c

3. a

4. a

5. d

6. d

Indonesia (page 43)
Evaluate the Map

1. Indonesia

2. The cities and natural features of the islands of Indonesia

3. political boundaries, land and water features, key, scale, compass rose, latitude and longitude, towns or cities

4. northern, southern, eastern

5. 12°S to 20°N; 95°E to 141°E

6. 9/16":200 mi or 9 mm:200 km

7. answers will vary

8. answers will vary

9. Pacific Ocean

10. accept all reasonable responses

Activity Page

1. c

2. a

3. c

4. d

5. b

6. b